TWENTY-FOUR LITTLE

FRENCH DINNERS

AND HOW TO COOK
AND SERVE THEM

BY CORA MOORE

24 Little French Dinners: And How to Cook and Serve Them.
By Cora Moore

Published by Arrow North, LLC in 2021 with a new interior design, hand-drawn illustrations, and introduction.

This book was originally published in 1919 by Cora Moore and E.P. Dutton & Company New York.

P art travel journal and cookbook, Cora Moore's *Twenty-Four Little French Dinners: And How to Cook and Serve Them* is a truly enjoyable read. Cooking and writing in 1919, Ms. Moore was well ahead of her time, predating famous later chefs like Julia Child. She shared the same mission; to erase the myth French recipes are too complex for American cooks.

Ms. Moore's writings and her recipes remain relevant today, as does her deep knowledge of France and the dishes the country is proud of. While we cannot find any biography of Ms. Moore, we can share in her passion for French food, its people, and French cookery. Perhaps she lived in France for some time and was exposed to a variety of foods, chefs, cooking at home, and their delightful open markets. Perhaps she was driven to develop dinner menus for American households to enjoy French food within a typical American family's limit of economy and of their time. Most of all, her drive to push American cooks out of their comfort zones by presenting them with these twenty-four little French menus shines through. We're excited to share them with you, in this annotated and beautifully-illustrated edition.

Arrow North, LLC
April 2021

An Important 2021 Safety Disclaimer. If you are interested in cooking the following dinners or recipes, keep in mind Cora Moore wrote *Twenty-Four Little French Dinners: And How to Cook and Serve Them* in 1919.

References to oven, heat, and stove may not be fueled by gas and electricity — they could be fueled by wood or coal-fired. Not every household had modern stoves in 1919. There are no references to cooking degrees, rather terms like high heat, very hot, simmer, and more. Also, measurements, as we are accustomed to today, are rarely mentioned in the book.

It is the reader's responsibility to determine the safety of the preparation of any of Ms. Moore's recipes. As the recipes are from 1919, use your discretion to thoroughly read (and re-read) to understand the preparation and ensure you aren't allergic to any of the ingredients.

The recipes presented are intended for entertainment and/or informational purposes and for use by persons having appropriate technical skill, at their own discretion and risk. Ms. Moore's recipes in this book have **not** been tested, and if should you desire to follow the recipes or make modifications to them, you are doing so at your own risk. The publisher, Arrow North, LLC is not responsible and does not assume obligation for the above and:

1. Adverse reactions or allergies to food consumed such as food poisoning and any kind of food-borne disease.
2. Misinterpreted recipes.
3. Domestic accidents, including but not limited to fires in your kitchen, injuries, or damage to property.
4. Warranties for the outcome of your food experiments.

TABLE OF CONTENTS

    Potage à la Duchesse
    Cabillaud à la Béchamel
    Pommes de Terre, Genevoise
    Salade Céleri
    Pouding à la vanille

    Consommé à la Napolitaine
    Cabillaud à la Financière
    Pommes de Terre en Rubans
    Beignets à la Printemps
    Choufleur au Gratin
    Bavaroise au Café

    Filet de Sole à la Provençal
    Poulet Sauté à l'Estragon
    Artichauts à la Barigoule
    Petit Petac
    Soufflé Georgette

Preface from the Author

The Little Dinners of Paris are world-famous. No one can have sojourned in the fascinating capital in its normal days without having come under their spell. To Parisien and visitor alike they are accounted among the uniquely characteristic features of the city's routine life.

Much of the interest that attaches to them is, of course, due to local atmosphere, to the associations that surround the quaint restaurants, half hidden in unexpected nooks and by-ways, to the fact that old Jacques "waits" in his shirtsleeves or that Grosse Marie serves you with a smile as expansive as her own proportions, or that it is Justin or François or "Old Monsoor," with his eternal grouch, who glides about the zinc counter.

But there is also magic in the arrangement of the menus, in the combinations of food, in the very names of the confections and in the little Gallic touches that, simple though they are, transform commonplace dishes into gastronomic delights.

There is inspiration in the art that enters into the production of a French dinner, in the perfect balance of every item from hors d'oeuvre to café noir, in the ways with seasoning that work miracles with left-overs and preserve the daily routine of three meals a day from the deadly monotony of the American regime, in the garnishings that glorify the most insignificant concoctions into objects of appetising beauty and in the sauces that elevate indifferent dishes into the realm of creations and enable a French cook to turn out a dinner fit for capricious young gods from what an American cook wastes in preparing one.

The very economy of the French is an art, and there is art in their economy. It is true that their dishes, as we have known them in this country, are expensive, even extravagant, but that is because they have been for the most part the creations of high-priced chefs. They who have made eating an avocation know that it is not necessary to dine expensively in order to dine well.

C. M.
New York, May 1919.

The Bugbear of American Cookery: **Monotony**

It is as strange as it is true that with the supplies that have lately proved sufficient to feed a world to draw upon the chief trouble with American cookery is its monotony. The American cook has a wider variety of foods at his command than any other in the world, yet in the average home how rarely is it that the palate is surprised with a flavor that didn't have its turn on the corresponding day last week or tickled with a sauce that is in itself an inspiration and a delight, not a mere "gravy," liable to harden into lumps of grease when it cools.

Most of this is simply the result of blindly following tradition. Daughter has accepted mother's precepts, regarding them even as the law of the Medes and the Persians, "which altereth not," and if it were not that increased prices and, lately, at least, "food regulations," have veritably compelled her toward a more wholesome simplicity, the United States would probably be what it was called half a generation ago, "a nation of dyspeptics." And we were a nation of dyspeptics because the great American mother of the latter end of the Nineteenth Century, in spite of all her unequaled qualities in every other direction, and in spite of all the encomiums she received in resounding prose or ecstatic verse for her prowess in the kitchen, was from the points of view of health, economy and wisdom the worst cook in the world.

With prices as they are the American housewife cannot afford to use butter and eggs and flour with the prodigality that was a habit with her mother, but so limited is the average woman's knowledge of cookery that these restrictions merely mean more monotony than ever. It is partly to demonstrate that this state of things is unnecessary, and that true food economy is not at all synonymous with "going without" that this book has been compiled.

It is upon variety that the French cook confidently relies to make each dish of each meal not just something to eat because her family must have food, not merely a sop to the Cerberus-gnawings of hunger, but a delight to the eye, to the palate, to the stomach truly a consummation devoutly to be wished for the American home table, and just as possible to attain as it is possible to procure from the grocer or the nearest pharmacist the ingredients by which these wonders are wrought.

But the average American woman doesn't look beyond her own kitchen and her own traditional row of spice boxes for her flavorings. She has her "kitchen set," which ordinarily comprises a row of little receptacles labeled "pepper," "salt," "cloves," "allspice," "ginger," "cinnamon," "nutmeg," and possibly one or two other spices or condiments—rarely more. With these and a bottle each of lemon extract and vanilla, she is satisfied that she is fully equipped as far as flavoring possibilities are concerned.

If she has laid in a box of sage and one of mixed dressing with, perhaps, some paprika and thyme, she views her fore sightedness with much complacency. She is supplied with savories.

Then she goes right on sighing, "Oh, for a new meat, instead of the same old round of mutton, pork, beef and fish; fish, beef, mutton and pork," disclaiming utterly any responsibility for the monotony that is undermining the family health and temper and, quite possibly, its morals.

That is where the American housewife makes her primary and most important mistake.

The French, on the other hand, know that there are, literally, hundreds of ways to vary every dish, however ordinary it may be in its primary state. That is their secret of success: unfailing variety coupled with economy.

However, this is not to claim that the American palate would take kindly to all the French cooks' little delicacies, or that it could be cultivated to that degree that makes a Frenchman regard a perfectly balanced meal even as an inspired poem. Probably Americans, as a class, could never be induced to eat some of the little birds—the mauviettes, the alouettes, the sparrows baked in a pie, that so delight the Frenchman. Also, it is a question whether snails, even if it were possible to obtain the superior Burgundian, fat and juicy and cooked even as our own Oscar used to prepare them for certain Waldorf guests, would ever appeal to the American taste, as even the common hedgerow sort of snail does to the average Frenchman.

It is not that the French dinners of Monte Carlo are necessarily so superior to American shore dinners, or that the little dinners of Paris are so infinitely to be pre-ferred to those, say, of certain places in New Orleans, or that the coppery-tasting oysters of Havre are to be compared with those of our own Baltimore. There is no more to

---

The American cook has a wider variety of foods at his command than any other in the world, yet in the average home how rarely is it that the palate is surprised with a flavor that didn't have its turn on the corresponding day last week or tick-led with a sauce that is in itself an inspiration and a delight, not a mere "gravy," liable to harden into lumps of grease when it cools.

---

be said, probably, for the woodcock pates of old Montreuil, or the rillettes of Tours, or the little pots of custard one gets at the foreign Montpelier, or the vol-au-vent, which is the pride and boast of the cities of Provence, than there is for grandmother's cookies such as have put Camden, Maine, on the map, or Lady Baltimore cakes, or the chicken pies one goes to northern New Hampshire to find in their glory, or the turkeys that, as much as the Green Mountains, make Vermont's fame.

Still, there is no question but that the American palate would benefit much by being cultivated, not only in the interests of economy, but also with a view to the increase of gastronomic pleasure, for a taste attuned to many variations is as an ear sensitive to the nuances of sweet sounds or an eye trained to perceive delicate tones and tints. It is really a matter for regret that we, as a people, have not been as willing to learn from the French the art of cooking and eating as we have been to acquire from them knowledge of the art of dress. Until we widen our horizon sufficiently to do this, we have not even begun to develop all our food resources or to understand the first principles of true food economy which is not at all synonymous with "going without."

But the average American woman doesn't look beyond her own kitchen and her own traditional row of spice boxes for her flavorings. She has her "kitchen set," which ordinarily comprises a row of little receptacles labeled "pepper," "salt," "cloves," "allspice," "ginger," "cinnamon," "nutmeg," and possibly one or two other spices or condiments—rarely more.

Flavor: *Handmaid of Variety*

I t is because he has a multitude of seasonings at his command and knows how to use them that the French cook is enabled not only to send to the table an infinite variety of dishes, but, at the same time, to practice economies that were otherwise impossible. The American buys an expensive cut of meat and, as is right in such a case, treats it as plainly and simply as possible. The Frenchman buys meat of a much lower quality, but so embellishes it that when it comes to the table it is superior, or, at least, equal to that which costs much more. It may be objected that this is no real economy, because by the time the French cook has sauced and spiced his cheap cut in order to make it palatable, the cost is as great, if not greater than it would have been had he paid more for his meat in the first place. This would be true enough according to the average American's method of procedure. But it is to be remembered that the French cook has already in his kitchen the cooking vinegars, the spices, the dried herbs, the extracts, that in very small amounts—a dash or a few leaves—are used at a time; also, that in a great number of cases, gravies and sauces are made from the by-products of the main dishes—those by-products that in the American kitchen usually go down the sink-drain or into the garbage pail.

Take a peep into the typical French cupboard. There you will find from twenty-five to thirty liquid seasonings such as anchovy extract, tabasco sauce, meat extracts, mushroom catsup, tomato paste, chutney, various vinegars, Worcestershire and many another flavoring designed to give a tang and a zest even to the most unpromising dish, if used aright. There you will find, too, fifty or more dry seasonings, including anise, basil, saffron, savoury, clove or garlic, cassia buds, bay leaf, ginger root, pepper-corns, marjoram, mint, thyme, capers and so on.

If (the French cook) uses garlic in a salad, it doesn't necessarily follow that the entire household must take on the atmosphere of an Italian barber shop, for he uses garlic or onion, not to give their flavor to a dish, but to bring out the flavors of the vegetables with which they are used.

Herein lie the "secrets" of French cookery which are, in truth, not secrets at all, but merely the application of common sense to the cuisine. The French have never, allowed their taste to be restricted by prejudice, so they hail a new flavor with delight rather than registering an instinctive dislike because it is not familiar. With a little applied education, Americans can bring the charm of the French table to their own homes rather than when they are, as they say, tired of the same old round of "eats," seeking out a nondescript table d'hote restaurant and eagerly consuming what is set before them, grateful for a change.

But don't harden your heart against French cookery merely because you have sampled it, as you fondly think, at one or another of the "red-inkeries" of New York or any other city. For the most part the "French" restaurants of the land are in reality not French at all, but Italian for the most part, and whatever Gallic flavor the remainder ever possessed has well-nigh vanished. There may be exceptions but, if there are, their patrons carefully guard the secret.

But to return to our subject: It is the French cook's knowledge of the subtleties, the nuances of seasoning that stands him in good stead. The American woman who has essayed to use some spice or savory unfamiliar to her and has turned out a dish which her family has declared "tasted like medicine" is, naturally enough, discouraged from wandering after that particular strange god again. The truth is that she has overdone the seasoning. She doesn't want to be parsimonious, which is just what the French cook is with his flavors, only he, more scientifically, calls it using good judgment. If he uses garlic in a salad, it doesn't necessarily follow that the entire household must take on the atmosphere of an Italian barber shop, for he uses garlic or onion, not to give their flavor to a dish, but to bring out the flavors of the vegetables with which they are used.

Vanilla and lemon have an almost universal appeal to the palate, and knowing this, the American cook, like the generation before her, has always seasoned her rice puddings, for instance, with one or the other, just as her apple sauce has invariably been flavored with lemon or nutmeg, her bread pudding with vanilla, and so all along her restricted line.

The French cook holds no brief against vanilla, and sometimes he flavors his rice pudding with it, but he so guides matters that the very sight or mention of rice pudding does not bring the thought of vanilla to the mind, for with him it may be flavored with pistache or rose or have a geranium leaf baked in it, giving a delightful, indescribable flavor. An ordinary bread pudding becomes veritably a queen of puddings as, indeed, it is called, merely by having a layer of jam through its center and a simple icing spread over the top. Ordinary pea soup exhibits chameleon-like possibilities merely through the addition of a little celeryroot, a dash of curry or the admixture of a few spoonfuls of minced spinach, and tomato soup has for most an appeal that even this favorite of soups never had before when just the right amount of thyme is added while it simmers, along with, perhaps a bayleaf.

But it is to be remembered that the French cook has already in his kitchen the cooking vinegars, the spices, the dried herbs, the extracts, that in very small amounts—a dash or a few leaves—are used at a time; also, that in a great number of cases, gravies and sauces are made from the by-products of the main dishes—those by-products that in the American kitchen usually go down the sink-drain or into the garbage pail.

In the recipes appended to the little dinners in this book a great many of the French cooks' materials are methods of procedure are set forth. But if the ordinarily experimental American housewife has the flavorings on hand, she will doubtless herself contrive many an alluring dish of her own. Variety is said to be the spice of life. However, that may be, the spices and their friends, the herbs, certainly make for variety in that important function of life, the dinner table.

True Trails Toward **Economy**

In the first place, no trail toward economy in conducting the cuisine of a household lies through the delicatessen store or the "fancy" grocery. It is an unflattering comment on the spirit of thrift of American housewives that the delicatessen store has settled down to such a flourishing existence, particularly in Eastern cities. Any woman who possesses a stove and a kitchen of her own should be ashamed to admit the laziness that more than a semi-occasional visit to these "delicate eating" places predicates. There are few things to be had in them that she shouldn't be able to make better at home and at a cost that is but a fraction of what she has to pay for the usually inferior, impersonal messes that come ready-made.

If the housewife has read some of the very excellent instructions that were printed to help her conduct her household adequately amid the necessary limitations of wartime, she already knows that there is absolutely no excuse for ever throwing away a crust or crumb of bread. As for that, neither is there any excuse for ever disposing of what is left of the morn ng cereal except to the advantage of some later made dish, or of consigning meat scraps or bits of fat or even bones to the garbage pail. It is not only that, in the interests of economy, she should use them; it is rather that if she is a good cook, she will be very glad to have them to use. Stale bread and breadcrumbs are the bases of a score of the most delicious puddings on the French cook's card; cooked cereal is one of the best thickenings for soups and gravies, as well as being far more wholesome than flour for this purpose; meat scraps, trimmings and bones should go into the stock pot. When a soup made of these is served as the introductory course at dinner it will be found that the family will be fully satisfied with much less meat, and it is in the lessening dependence of Americans on meat that will make for the greatest item in economy.

A French cook of parts would tear his hair if he could see how fats and drippings from meats are thrown away in many an American kitchen. They are poured into the sink till the drainpipes clog and, to complete the little serial of extravagance, the plumber has to be called. The French cook knows that this is the finest grease for frying in the world and that its use would save many a pound of butter. He strains it all carefully and keeps the different sorts in labelled jars or crocks. He knows by experience what particular fats give the best flavors to certain things, and he knows that vegetables, fish, eggs, pancakes and what not are far better fried in these natural fats. Who that ever ate an egg fried in bacon drippings will ever want one cooked in butter, even at a dollar a pound!

One will not find the delicatessen flourishing in France—one will not find it at all—and the fancy grocery, above mentioned, is another pitfall for the American housewife. She likes the sight of food done up in fancy containers, in glass, perhaps, and buys them, not realizing that she is paying a large price for perfectly unnecessary and totally unnourishing "pretties." If she is fearful of the handling some loose food stuffs may be subjected to in the stores, why does she not practice the most practical economy, go to the fountain-head of supplies in the city, the large market, and buy in quantity, so far as she can? A few ounces of bacon, already sliced, and sealed in a glass dish are, indeed, appetising even in their raw state, while a side of bacon is not, unless looked upon through the eyes of imagination, yet the latter method of purchasing this commodity is two or three hundred per cent cheaper, and when it arrives at the breakfast table it will be found every bit as appealing to a happy morning appetite.

Any consideration of economy in the cuisine must include the meat problem. Meat is the most expensive item on the menu and the true solution of the question is not only to conserve all the uses of it but to eat much less. That would make not only for economy, but for better health as well. It has been estimated that 186 pounds of dressed meat is—or was prior to the war—the yearly average of consumption for

A French cook of parts would tear his hair if he could see how fats and drippings from meats are thrown away in many an American kitchen. They are poured into the sink till the drainpipes clog and, to complete the little serial of extravagance, the plumber has to be called.

every American; the Englishman being a good second with his 120 pounds, while the Frenchman remained perfectly contented and healthy with 79 pounds, the Italian with 72 pounds, and the Swiss, anything but a nation of invalids, managed very well on 60 pounds per person.

This is no plea for vegetarianism, though it may be said in passing for the benefit of those who think that good red blood and hardy muscle are to be obtained only by absorbing the red blood and muscle of the beasts of the field, that there is as much, if not more, of this building power in the beans, the peas, the lentils that we regard too often as mere secondary foods.
Most of all the American should take advantage of the great stores of fish which are equally as nourishing as meat and may easily be made as appetising with simple sauces that French cookery will teach us. Fish are cheap; at least, many neglected kinds are; they are easy to cook and they are one of the best foods in the world.

The **Appeal** *to the Eye*

No one, least of all the French cook, calculates to feast the eye at the expense of the sense of taste, yet it is his experience after long years that good digestion is much more likely to wait upon the appetite that has been stirred to a preliminary enthusiasm by the attractive appearance of a dish. So, they serve little fritters of vegetables, dabs of jelly, slices of hard boiled eggs, pickles, parsley, cress and nasturtiums with meats, put sprigs of fresh green in their gravies, decorate desserts with nut-meats, flowers and fruits, and in so doing add a bit to the gayety of the table, satisfied that the trifling extra expense, time and energy incurred is more than compensated for in the pleasure the results afford. A fair trial of this pleasant idiosyncrasy of the French is convincing that the appearance of a dish has more bearing on the relish of a meal than we over here have fully realized.

They are particular, however, to be consistent in the use of garnishing's. Flowers and fruits are reserved for sweet dishes, except in the case of nasturtiums, which they regard as much a vegetable as a flower and use freely with meats.

A stew or a creamed dish is merely a more or less indifferent something to eat when it is dished up any old way and set upon the table. But if it is heaped daintily on a pretty platter, surrounded by a ring of brown mashed potato, its sides decorated by dainty shapes of toasted bread, perhaps buttered and sprinkled with minced parsley, it has become something to awaken the slumbering or indifferent appetite and at practically no extra expense of time or money. If the yolks of two hard boiled eggs are minced and mixed with part of the raw white of one, the paste then formed into balls like marbles and dropped into boiling water, one has little yellow spheres to lend an enlivening color note to clear soups. Two or three of these dropped into each plate just before serving makes a pleasing change from the usual croutons.

Sprigs of fresh chickory make the daintiest of garnishes for cold meats, and a few of the tender green stalks will add to the appearance of practically any salad. As for water-cress and pepper-grass and, of course, parsley, minced and otherwise, no French chef would think of preparing a meal without a plentiful supply of them on hand.

It isn't essential that every dish should be turned into an elaborate work of art, as if it were to be entered at the annual exhibition of the Société des Chefs de Cuisine, but neither is there any reason, even with modest means at command, for giving cause for that old slogan of the great American dinner table: "It tastes better than it looks."

Sauces: *Simple and Otherwise*

Brillat-Savarin, who would be remembered as a wit had he not been even more brilliant as a chef, paid his respects to the English by saying they were a nation of a hundred religions and only one sauce. Being a true Frenchman, he believed a reversal of the numbers better for the soul. It is certainly better for the appetite.

To be sure the proper mental sauce for a good dinner is wit, and the best physical one, hunger, but as we all of us have more or less of an Epicurean strain in us and do not eat solely to satisfy bodily needs, it is well that the American cook who essays to bring variety to her board should have some knowledge of those Gallic creations, the sauces, by which she is enabled to transform plain dishes into seemingly pretentious ones, even though she never attain that sauce that Balzac knew, "in which a mother might unsuspectingly eat her own child."

ROUX

In the first place every French chef keeps three kinds of what he calls roux on hand, ready for making meat and fish sauces. These are made by cooking together eight ounces of butter and nine ounces of flour. That intended for use with brown meats is stirred together till it becomes a medium brown in shade; white roux is cooked only sufficiently to banish the raw taste and not allowed to color, while pale roux is kept over the fire just long enough to attain a deep cream color. These are mixed with milk, soup stock, water or gravy as the case may be when a sauce for fish, meat or vegetables is needed.

SAUCE À LA CRÈME

For instance, to make Sauce à la Crème, for use with white entries, take two tablespoonfuls of the white roux in a saucepan with a cup of milk and a tablespoonful each of finely chopped parsley, shallots and chives. Boil fifteen minutes, pass through a colander into another saucepan, add a small lump of butter, more finely chopped parsley and salt and pepper. Mix well with a wooden spoon and it is ready for the table.

SAUCE PIQUANTE

To make a favorite Sauce Piquante, cut two onions into slices, also a carrot and two shallots and put into a saucepan with a scant tablespoonful of butter. While heating over a moderate fire, add a sprig of thyme, a tablespoonful of minced parsley, a bayleaf and two or three cloves. When the onions are golden brown add a tablespoonful of flour, a little plain stock and a tablespoonful of vinegar. Boil again, pass through a sieve and season with salt and pepper.

SAUCE MAÎTRE D'HÔTEL

A simple sauce is that Maître d'Hôtel, which is rarely made at home though so generally liked. Put a lump of butter into a small saucepan over a moderate fire and add to it chopped parsley and chives, or parsley alone. Season with salt and pepper and a little lemon juice and while it is sizzling pour over the hot steak or fish.

SAUCE D'ANCHOIS

Sauce d'Anchois, than which there isn't anything better with baked fish, is also easy to make. Take three or four anchovies and mash them up well with two tablespoonfuls of butter. Now make about a pint of brown sauce with brown roux and milk, and stir the anchovy butter into it. Just before taking from the fire add the juice of half a lemon or more, according to taste.

SAUCE BEARNAISE

Sauce Bearnaise was a favorite of Henry of Navarre, and it is excellent with steaks, chops and, particularly, roast beef. To make it beat the yolks of three or four eggs in a saucepan, add a tablespoonful of butter and a little salt. Stir over a slow fire till the eggs begin to thicken, then remove and stir in two more tablespoonfuls of butter, stirring till the butter is dissolved. Season with chopped fine herbs and parsley and pour in a teaspoonful of French vinegar.

SAUCE RAVIGOTE

In many parts of France, they have a favorite dressing for boiled fish called Sauce Ravigote. To make it mix half a pint of stock in a saucepan with a small amount of white wine or cider, then chop fine herbs such as chervil, tarragon, chives and parsley, or whatever other herbs are in season, to the amount of about three tablespoonfuls, and mix with the stock, adding salt and pepper. Stew gently for about twenty minutes, then blend a tablespoonful each of flour and butter, stir into the sauce and continue to stir till thick. Just before serving squeeze in the juice of half a lemon. The word "Ravigote" means, literally, "pick me up," and it is applied to minced tarragon, chervil, chives and parsley, the herbs being kept separate and served with salad on four little saucers. Ravigote butter, made by kneading butter with the four herbs and adding pepper, salt and lemon juice, spread between thin slices of bread, makes delicious sandwiches.

SAUCE BLANQUETTE

To make the very generally liked Sauce Blanquette, which is used to raise cold meats to the dignity of a fricassee, take about four ounces of pale mux, thin slightly with boiling water added by degrees, then put in a bunch of sweet herbs, cooked button mushrooms and small onions and pepper and salt to taste. Put in whatever cold meat you have, cook till it is well heated and serve.

SAUCE D'HAVRE

The following is called Sauce d'Havre, and through the use of it will be discovered that the taste of curry is an agreeable one in many another case than in connection with the veal and rice arrangement to which most American cooks restrict it. Peel and slice four onions and two apples and place in a stewpan with four ounces of butter, six peppercorns, a sprig of thyme, two bayleaves and a blade of mace. When the onions have become slightly brown over the moderate fire, stir in a mixture of two tablespoonfuls of flour and the same amount of curry powder, shortly afterward adding six gills of white stock and half a pint of white sauce. Season with salt and half a teaspoonful of moist sugar, boil for a quarter of an hour, adding more white stock if necessary, and stirring constantly. Put through a strainer into another saucepan, boil up again, skim, and use when required.

SAUCE LYONS

Fricasseed chicken takes on a new glory when it is prepared with Sauce Lyons. This is made by stirring gradually three well-beaten eggs into half a pint of plain white sauce, then placing the mixture in a jar and standing in boiling water till the sauce thickens. Just prior to pouring over the chicken add the strained juice of half a lemon.

Brillat-Savarin, who would be remembered as a wit had he not been even more brilliant as a chef, paid his respects to the English by saying they were a nation of a hundred religions and only one sauce.

Twenty-Four Little French Dinners

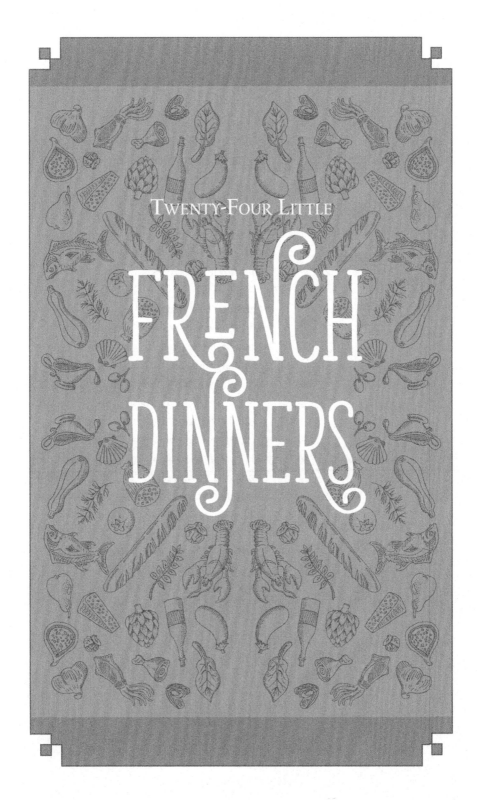

TWENTY-FOUR LITTLE

FRENCH DINNERS

CORA MOORE

MENU 1

Potage à la Duchesse
Cabillaud à la Béchamel
Pommes de Terre, Genevoise
Salade Céleri
Pouding à la vanille

Potage à la Duchesse.
Butter a baking sheet, cover with four ounces of chou paste, cook in the oven for six minutes, then cover the paste with forcemeat in small lumps, a little distance apart. Cut the paste into twelve equal sized pieces, each piece holding a lump of the forcemeat, place in a tureen, pour over a quart of piping hot consommé and serve.

Cabillaud à la Béchamel.
Mix an ounce of flour with an ounce and a half of butter melted in a saucepan, then gradually add a pint of milk which has been allowed previously to simmer with a minced onion and carrot in it, also a bunch of sweet herbs, two or three cloves, a grating of nutmeg and pepper and salt. Bring to a boil, add two or three tablespoonfuls of cream, strain and put back into the saucepan. Now put in two or three pounds of cod, previously boiled and flaked, being thoroughly free from skin and bones. Shake all together very gently and when all is thoroughly hot, turn out onto a silver dish and garnish with sliced hard-boiled eggs.

Pommes de Terre, Genevoise.

Shred four medium sized boiled potatoes, season with a little salt and pepper. Butter lightly half a dozen tartlet moulds, cover the bottoms with grated Parmesan cheese, arrange in each a layer of potatoes, then another sprinkling of cheese, and so on till the moulds are filled. Put a little butter on top. Place on a very hot stove or in a very hot oven for fifteen minutes to half an hour. Serve on a hot dish in the moulds.

Salade Celeri.

Trim two or three heads of celery, cut into short shreds, wash thoroughly in cold water and drain. Place in a salad bowl, season with a little salt, a very little pepper and one or two tablespoonfuls each of oil and vinegar. Add several sprigs of peppergrass and serve at once.

Pouding à la Vanille.

Place a vanilla bean in a mortar together with half a pound of sugar and pound well together and sift. Separate the whites from the yolks of three eggs, beat the yolks well, stir them in with a pint of cream and mix in with the vanilla sugar. Whisk the whites of the eggs to a stiff froth and mix lightly in with the other ingredients. Butter a pudding mould, pour in the mixture and cover with a sheet of oiled paper. Stand the mould in a saucepan of boiling water and steam the pudding for half an hour. In the meantime, prepare the following sauce: Pour a breakfast cupful of canned or fresh pineapple juice into a lined pan with the juice of a lemon. Put this on the fire till it boils, then pour it over a tablespoonful of arrowroot, stirring all the time. Return the sauce to the saucepan and stir till it thickens over the fire. When the pudding is cooked, turn it out onto a hot dish, strain the sauce over it and serve. Be careful that no water enters the mould containing the pudding while it is cooking, or it will be spoiled.

MENU 2

Consommé à la Napolitaine
Cabillaud à la Financière
Pommes de Terre en Rubans
Beignets à la Printemps
Choufleur au Gratin
Bavaroise au Café

Consommé à la Napolitaine.
Place in a saucepan with a lump of butter equal quantities of finely minced carrots, turnips, a head of lettuce and one of endive with a little chervil. Add a quart of the water in which the cauliflower in this dinner was cooked, pepper and salt, and simmer for an hour. Just before serving stir in the beaten yolk of an egg and half a pint of milk.

Cabillaud à la Financière.
Cook a piece of cod weighing three pounds in salted water for twenty minutes, drain a place on a serving platter covered with the following sauce: Put two glasses of Madeira wine and a small piece of meat glaze in a saucepan with a pint of Spanish sauce and a gill each of essence of mushrooms and truffles. Boil till it coats the spoon.

Pommes de Terre en Rubans.
Take large, smooth, pared potatoes and cut round and round in spirals about an eighth of an inch thick. Keep covered with a damp napkin till all are cut, place in a frying basket and fry in very hot fat till a light straw color. Sprinkle freely with salt and serve immediately.

Beignets à la Printemps.

Make a sauce of two ounces of butter, four ounces of flour, a tablespoonful of brandy, a pinch of salt, sufficient water to make a creamy paste. Cook and, removing from the stove, work in the whites of two eggs beaten to a stiff froth. Cut into pieces any fruit desired, dip them in the batter and fry in butter to a light golden brown. Drain well, place in a serving dish, sprinkle well with powdered sugar and serve. If the fruit is not fully ripe, parboil in syrup before using.

Choufleur au Gratin.

Soak a cauliflower in water with plenty of salt, then boil in plenty of salted water for fifteen minutes. Remove and take away all the green leaves, lay it on a flat buttered dish, previously rubbed with an onion, and pour over it a sauce made as follows: Melt an ounce and a half of butter in a saucepan, add a dessertspoonful of flour, mix and add a cup of milk. Stir till it thickens, add pepper and salt and add two or three tablespoonfuls of grated Parmesan cheese. Mix well and after pouring over the cauliflower sprinkle all over with breadcrumbs and place the dish in the oven till nicely browned.

Bavaroise au Café.

Mix the beaten yolks of two eggs with a pint of milk and a cup of very strong black coffee. Bring to a boil in a saucepan, remove from the fire and allow to get cold, stirring occasionally. Add the yolks of two more eggs beaten stiff with two ounces of sugar. Mix well and then add the stiffly beaten whites of the four eggs along with half an ounce of dissolved gelatin. Pour into a mould and turn out when set.

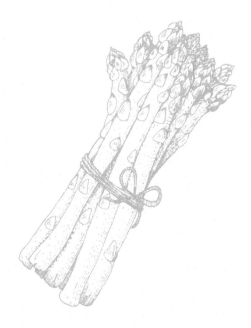

MENU 3

Filet de Sole à la Provençal
Poulet Sauté à l'Estragon
Artichauts à la Barigoule
Petit Petac
Soufflé Georgette

Filets des Soles à la Provençal.
Sprinkle the filets with pepper and salt and a little allspice and fry in salad oil with a finely chopped onion and a little chopped parsley. Serve with a slice of lemon on each filet.

Poulet Sauté à l'Estragon.
Sprinkle the pieces of a cut up raw chicken with pepper and salt and cook in a saucepan with a little oil. Make a gravy of a cupful of clear stock in which tarragon stalks have been boiled for an hour, dish up the fowl on a hot platter, pour over the sauce, straining it, and sprinkle on top tarragon leaves blanched and coarsely chopped.

Artichauts à la Barigoule.
Cut off the tops and leaves of the artichokes and boil the bottoms in plenty of slightly salted water till tender. Scoop out the fibrous interior. Grate some cooked bacon into a saucepan with a gill of fine herbs and a cupful of broth. Cook for five minutes. Put a little of this mixture in each artichoke, cover the opening with a slice of lemon and bake in a sauté-pan in the oven for twenty minutes.

Petit Petac.
Peel tiny new potatoes and sauté in oil till
a golden brown. Sprinkle with chopped
parsley and serve.

Soufflé Georgette.
Grate a half-dozen stale macaroons into
a half-cup of brandy, add a pint of cream
and two teaspoonfuls of dissolved gelatine.
Whip in a dozen maraschino cherries and
turn into a mould to harden. Serve with
macaroons dipped into the liquid that
comes around the maraschino cherries. A
custard may be used in this recipe instead of
the cream.

MENU 4

Potage au Riz
Rougets en Papillotes
Veau à la Suzette
Demi tasse

Potage au Riz.

Put half a pound of well-washed rice into a saucepan with two quarts of vegetable stock and boil till tender. When the rice is cooked move the saucepan to the side of the fire and mix in a cupful of stewed tomatoes and an ounce and a half of butter. Serve with sippets of toast or croutons that have been fried in butter.

Rougets en Papillotes.

This recipe is for mullets, but any small, plump fish may be used. Make a paper case for each fish with a sheet of well-oiled notepaper and put the cases into the oven for a few minutes to harden. Sprinkle the under sides of the fish with pepper and salt and lay them in their cases with a small piece of butter under and over each. Place the cases in a baking dish and cook for about twenty minutes in the oven, or more if the fish are otherwise than small. Sprinkle well with lemon juice just before serving.

Veau à la Suzette.

Trim saddle of veal neatly and put it into a
saucepan with a good sized piece of butter.
Turn it constantly on the fire till it is a rich
golden color all over, then put it onto a
dish and sprinkle with salt and pepper. Add
more butter to the gravy in the saucepan
and put in raw potatoes cut up in sections
like oranges. Cover the saucepan and cook,
shaking frequently, till the potatoes have a
good color. Add an onion, finely minced,
and when it is browned, a clove of garlic,
minced very fine; next put in a tablespoonful of flour followed, when the flour is
brown, by about two cupfuls of stock. Stir
well and put back the meat and any juice
that may have oozed from it. Lastly add a
bouquet of herbs, simmer for an hour at
least and serve the meat surrounded by the
potatoes with the sauce poured over the
whole.

*Note: a Demi tasse recipe was not included
within the original copy of this book.*

MENU 5

Potage à l'Américaine
Filet d'Eglefin
Gigot de Mouton aux Epinards
Chou de Mer au Fromage
Petites Crèmes au Chocolat

Potage à l'Américaine.

Parboil a medium sized cauliflower in salted water, change the water and boil till done. Drain well and press through a sieve. Dilute with consommé or broth. Boil a few minutes more, stirring well. Beat up in a basin the yolk of an egg with three tablespoonfuls of cream, add this to a few tablespoonfuls of the cauliflower mixture, then, taking the saucepan containing the soup from the fire, add the egg and cream mixture and stir together. Add half an ounce of butter and serve with croutons.

Filet d'Eglefin.

Cut a haddock into fillets, trimming into pieces about six inches long. Dip them in well beaten egg and then into sifted bread-crumbs and plunge into deep, well-boiling fat, frying to a rich color, turning occasionally to cook both sides evenly. Remove, drain, put on a cloth spread over a hot dish and serve with a simple white sauce.

Gigot de Mouton aux Epinards.

Roast a small leg of mutton, putting some salt and a small quantity of water at the bottom of the tin. When half cooked, remove the meat and carefully skim the gravy of all fat. Return the mutton to the tin, pour gravy over it and surround it with potatoes cut to the size of walnuts. Put back in the oven, letting the potatoes cook in the juice of the meat. Meanwhile cook about three pounds of spinach, drain, squeeze out all water and pass through a sieve. Return to a saucepan in which about two ounces of butter has been heated and season with pepper and salt. Add a tablespoonful of gravy from the mutton and allow the spinach to simmer till the meat is done. Then pile the spinach with the potatoes about the meat and serve, having the gravy in a sauceboat.

Chou de Mer au Fromage.
Carefully wash sea-kale to remove grit, remove any black parts from the roots and tie up the shoots in small bundles. Cook in boiling salted water for twenty minutes, drain and keep hot. Mix on the fire an ounce of butter and a tablespoonful of flour, moisten with half a cup of water in which the kale was cooked, bring to a boil and mix in two or three tablespoonsfuls of grated Parmesan cheese. Take from the fire and add the beaten yolk of an egg. Arrange the kale on a hot dish, pour the sauce over and serve immediately.

Petites Crèmes au Chocolat.
Mix two tablespoonfuls of chocolate or cocoa in a cup of boiling milk and sweeten to taste. When nearly cold add to this the yolks of two eggs, well beaten, and a gill of heavy cream. Mix thoroughly and strain into china cases. Place these in a large shallow stewpan containing just sufficient water to reach halfway up on the cases. Let steam for twenty minutes, when the custard ought to be firm. The water should be boiling when the cases are first put in, but afterwards may simmer. Put the cases on ice, and serve as cold as possible with little sponge cakes or lady fingers.

MENU 6

Potage purée de Pois Secs
Saumon à la Hollandaise
Pommes de Terre, Barigoule
Haricots verts au riz tomate

Potage Purée de Pois Secs.

Boil a pint of green peas in three pints of water with a piece of fat ham or bacon, two carrots, an onion, a leek, a bayleaf, some parsley, pepper and salt. Allow to simmer two or three hours, stirring occasionally. Pass the peas and onions through a hair sieve and add the strained liquor. Return to the saucepan, boil up, add some whole cooked peas with a little mint and serve.

Saumon à la Hollandaise.

Cut a piece of salmon from the middle of the fish, cover in the kettle with cold water and, plenty of salt. Bring slowly to a boil, removing scum, and allow to simmer till the fish is done. Drain thoroughly and serve with the following sauce in a boat: Take three ounces of butter, the yolks of two eggs and put them in a double boiler over the fire, stirring briskly till the butter is dissolved. Mix in a scant ounce of flour, stir well and add the juice of a lemon, half a pint of milk, a little grated nutmeg and pepper and salt. Stir constantly till the sauce thickens to the consistency of a custard.

Pommes de Terre, Barigoule.

Place ten potatoes in a saucepan with
enough broth to cover them and boil slowly
till done. Drain, taking care not to break
them. Put a teacupful of olive oil into a
deep frying pan, heat, put in the potatoes,
tossing them till they are browned all over
lightly. Place on a dish and sprinkle with
salt, pepper and vinegar. Serve piping hot.

Haricots verts au riz tomate.

Boil rice carefully so that every grain will be
separate, toss it in a little butter and moist-
en with tomato sauce and add the yolk of
an egg, well beaten and stirred in, and a
little Parmesan cheese. Make a border of the
rice on a dish and pile in the center some
French beans plainly boiled and tossed in a
little butter with some pepper and salt.

MENU 7

Potage Velouté

Brochet à la Tartare

Biftecks sautés aux Olives

Pommes de Terre à la Lyonnaise

Épinards au Gratin

Beignets Soufflés

Potage Velouté.

Boil a cup and a half of tapioca in two quarts of water and season with salt and pepper. At the bottom of a tureen place a lump of butter, and the yolks of two eggs, pour the tapioca over while it is still boiling, add a pint of hot milk and serve.

Brochet à la Tartare.

Cut a fresh pike into slices and marinade each slice separately with a sauce made of sufficient olive oil, black pepper, a minced onion, finely cut mushrooms and chopped parsley. Cover the fish with breadcrumbs and broil, brushing occasionally with the marinade. When it is a golden color remove from the fire, place on a hot platter and serve sprinkled with parsley with a tartar sauce in a sauceboat.

Biftecks sautés aux Olives.

Cut the steak into six pieces and toss in a frying pan with lard. When well done sprinkle with seasoning and remove from the fire. Then take half a glass of white wine, a tablespoonful of consomme, two or three dozen green olives, with the pits removed, and boil together for a few minutes. Set the steak in a crown on the platter and in the center place the dressing. Pour the gravy from the frying pan over all and serve.

Pommes de Terre à la Lyonnaise.
Take a dozen potatoes of the same size, cut
into pieces the size of a quarter of a dollar,
roll in flour and put into a frying pan with
boiling fat, taking them out when they are
a golden brown. Also fry some thin slices of
onion, mix with the potatoes, sprinkle with
salt and serve garnished with parsley.

Épinards au Gratin.
Boil two pounds of spinach and chop very
fine. Beat up two eggs to each pound of
spinach, mix with it and sprinkle the whole
with breadcrumbs. Pour over some olive
oil or melted butter and heat thoroughly in
the oven in a vegetable dish.

Beignets Soufflés.
Put a pound of flour, a pinch of salt, a liquor
glass of rum, the yolks of three eggs and a
quantity of lukewarm water into a mixing
dish and beat these together till it shrinks
from the dish. Then mix in the well-beaten
whites of the eggs and then allow to rise for
an hour or so. Have a baking dish very hot
and put in the paste in pieces the size of a
nut, which will triple in size while cooking.
Let them cook to a golden color, remove
from the fire and sprinkle with powdered
sugar. Serve hot.

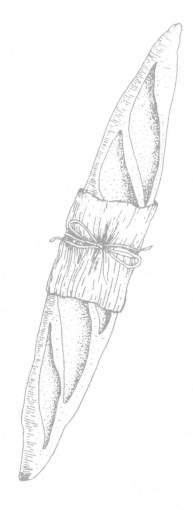

MENU 8

Consommé Royale
Filet de Sole à la Vénétienne
Salade Barbe de Capucin
Beignets de Pêches

Consommé Royale.
Beat two eggs and mix them with half a cup of milk and a pinch of salt. Pour into a basin, stand this in a larger one containing hot water, place in the oven and bake till the contents of the small basin are firm, renewing water in the larger dish if necessary. Allow to cool and when set cut into small well-shaped pieces, pour over them a quart of hot consommé and serve immediately.

Filet de Sole à la Vénétienne.
Place in a buttered tin two small or one large onion cut in thin slices, a little chopped parsley, a bayleaf, one or two whole cloves and salt and pepper. Lay the fillets of two soles on these with a generous piece of butter, pour over half a pint of white stock and a small glass of white wine. Cover the tin with oiled paper, and bake in the oven for about twelve minutes. When the fish is cooked take out all the liquor except just enough to keep the fish moist as it remains in the oven turned very low, strain it and add three-quarters of an ounce of flour and the same amount of butter. Bring the sauce to a boil, take it from the fire, add the yolk of an egg and a good amount of blanched parsley and chervil, chopped very fine. Arrange the fillets of sole on a hot dish, pour the sauce over and serve.

Salade Barbe de Capucin.

Carefully pick over and break into conve-
nient pieces the required amount of chicory
and place in a salad bowl well rubbed with
an onion. Just before serving pour over
a French dressing, remembering to be in
making it "a spendthrift for oil, a miser for
vinegar, a counselor for salt and a madman
to stir it all up."

Beignets des Pêches.

Peel, stone and cut in halves some firm
peaches. Toss about in a bowl with sugar,
being careful not to break. Put a pound of
flour in a basin and stir in gradually half a
pint of water. Mix the whites of two stiffly
beaten eggs with this batter and then add
one and a quarter ounce of melted butter.
Bring olive oil to a good heat in a frying
pan, dip each piece of peach in the batter
and fry in the fat. When lightly browned
drain on a cloth or paper, lay on a baking
dish, sift powdered sugar over and glaze
by placing in a hot oven a few minutes.
Arrange in pyramid shape on a folded
napkin on a hot dish and serve immediately. Canned peaches, if firm, may, of course,
be substituted for the fresh fruit.

MENU 9

*Côtelettes de Saumon, à
l'Anglaise
Pommes de Terre, Marquise
Petits Pois à la Paysanne
Salade Américaine
Choux au Chocolat*

Côtelettes de Saumon, Anglaise.
Divide slices of salmon into shape of cutlets,
sprinkle with pepper and salt and put into a
saucepan with a small amount of butter and
toss over the fire. When cooked take out and
drain, place on a hot dish and serve with the
following sauce: Put three tablespoonfuls of
velouté sauce into a saucepan, reduce slightly
and add one egg, four ounces of butter,
a little salt, cayenne, some finely minced
parsley and the juice of half a lemon. Mix
together well over the fire till the ingredients
are blended and it is ready.

Pommes de Terre, Marquise.
Boil potatoes in salted water and pass
through a sieve. Season with salt, pepper,
nutmeg, chopped parsley and a little chopped
thyme. Moisten with some good gravy or
stock and form into small balls. Dip each in
well beaten egg and fry to a light brown in
butter.

Petits Pois à la Paysanne.
Take fresh green peas, or canned ones if the
former are not available, put over the fire in
a saucepan with plenty of butter and stir frequently. Cut one or two rashers of bacon in
very small dice and toss them in a saucepan
over the fire. When the bacon is well fried,
mix in with the peas and let the two finish
cooking together, seasoning with pepper, salt
and a little sugar.

Salade Amèricaine.

Cut in rounds resembling a quarter-dollar
equal quantity of new potatoes, carrots and
beet root, all previously cooked. Then add
a sour apple, cut in the same shape, and
a few anchovies cut in small pieces. Pour
over this a dressing of three parts oil to
one of vinegar, add pepper, salt, mustard
and chopped parsley. Pile the salad up and
surround with cress.

Choux au Chocolat.

Into a small saucepan put half a cup of
water with two ounces of butter and one of
sugar. When boiling add gradually two and
a half ounces of finely sifted flour and stir
till the mixture is stiff. Take from the fire,
stir some more, then add two eggs, one at a
time, beat the whole well, and leave to cool.
Butter a baking sheet, lay the paste on it in
round balls the size of a plum and bake in
a moderate oven for about twenty minutes.
Allow to cool and then make an incision
in the side of each and fill with whipped
cream slightly flavored with vanilla or with
jam. Just before serving glaze each chou
slightly with a chocolate icing.

MENU 10

Consommé Duchesse

Saumon, Sauce Piquante

Rissolettes de Bœuf

Salade à la Reine

Crème Noyau

Duchesse Consommé.

Boil four tablespoonfuls of rice (ground) in four cups of water for fifteen minutes, adding half a teaspoonful each of salt and sugar. When the rice is soft and just before serving add a quart of warmed milk, bring to a boil, adding lastly a dash of pepper and paprika.

Saumon, Sauce Piquante.

Take slices of salmon about three-quarters of an inch in thickness and place in a saucepan with hot fish broth mixed with a small quantity of wine. Allow to simmer for fifteen minutes. When cooked remove and wipe free from broth, place on a hot platter and serve with a sauce made as follows: Melt a quantity of butter, flavor to taste with tarragon vinegar, pepper, mustard, fennel and such spices as are liked. Stir over the fire till cooked, move to the side of the stove, thicken with the yolk of an egg and serve.

Rissolettes de Boeuf.

With four cups of finely minced beef mix one cup of breadcrumbs, adding one boiled onion, a little essence of anchovies, salt, pepper and a raw egg. Make into balls, roll in breadcrumbs and fry slowly. Prepare a gravy by boiling the trimmings of the meat in the water in which the onion was boiled, thicken with flour or cornstarch, add three teaspoonfuls of lemon juice and pour over the rissolettes which should be arranged on a heated platter around a heap of mashed potatoes.

Salade à la Reine.

Lay strips of endive lengthwise on the salad plates and cross them with peeled tomatoes cut in sections like an orange. Dress with a French salad dressing.

Crème Noyau.

Pound in a mortar together a quarter pound of Jordan and an ounce of bitter almonds with a scant half cup of cream and two ounces of sugar. Rub through a sieve into a bowl, add a pint of whipped cream flavored with Noyau and then an ounce of gelatine dissolved. Pour into a mould to set. Serve with champagne wafers.

MENU 11

Consommé à la Madrilène
Perches aux Fines Herbes
Filets Mignons aux Pommes de Terre
Aubergines Farcies
Omelette au Rhum

Consommé à la Madrilène.
Put through a medium sieve five or six boiled ripe tomatoes, or a can of tomatoes, allow to cool and pack in a freezer. Add to a cold consommé and serve in cups.

Perches aux Fines Herbes.
Prepare six fresh perch and marinade them with two tablespoonfuls of olive oil, a sprig of parsley, a little pepper and salt and allspice, bayleaf and other strong spices chopped fine. Keep the fish in this for about an hour, remove and roll in bread- crumbs lightly flavored with spices. Grill over a low fire till a golden brown in color and serve with butter sauce.

Filets Mignons aux Pommes de Terre.
Marinade the required number of small filets mignon of mutton in butter seasoned with salt and chervil. Leave for an hour or more and just before they are to be served, grill them, basting frequently with the butter. Flavor with lemon juice and serve with buttered fried potatoes.

Aubergines Farcies.

Cut eggplants in halves lengthwise, remove
the inside and of this make a farcie by
mixing it with chopped parsley, two
chopped onions and salt and pepper. Stuff
the eggplant halves with this mixture
and put the combination into a casserole
containing a good quantity of melted
butter and allow to simmer over a slow fire
till all is thoroughly done. Cover the tops
with breadcrumbs, add a drop of oil or a
little melted butter and keep piping hot till
served.

Omelette au Rhum.

Prepare an omelette as for any sweet
omelette and just before serving place on a
hot platter, pour rum over, ignite and carry
to the table blazing.

MENU 12

Potage Biz, Creçy
Canapés de Saumon Fumé
Paupiettes de Porc, Sauce Piquante
Asperges en Petits Pois
Tarte à la Turque

Potage Riz, Crecy.
Cut several firm, red carrots lengthwise, using only the red part. Place in a casserole with a good bouillon and allow to simmer over a slow fire. Pass through a sieve when the carrots are soft, and put back in the bouillon. Add a cupful of cooked rice, bring to a boil and serve.

Canapés de Saumon Fumé.
Cut a smoked salmon into slices and spread them with butter, adding pepper and salt and a pinch of nutmeg. Heat over a crisp fire, place on a hot dish, cover with croutons and serve.

Paupiettes de Pore, Sauce Piquante.
Take small slices of cold roast pork and spread them with sausage meat. Roll them and fasten with skewers, then cover with a thin coating of lard or with oiled paper and cook them over a low fire in a casserole. When thoroughly done, take off the papers, cover with breadcrumbs and brown. Serve with a piquant sauce.

Asperges en Petits Pois.

Cut up the green part of two bunches of asparagus, roll in butter and add a little salt. Heat a cupful of flour, being careful not to allow it to color, and dredge the asparagus with it. Put into a saucepan with sufficient milk and water in equal parts to cover, add a bouquet of herbs and allow the whole to simmer till the asparagus is cooked. Season with white pepper and serve.

Tarte à la Turque.

Boil a cupful of rice till thick in milk to which has been added a stick of cinnamon, a little lemon juice and sugar. When the rice is cooked allow to cool. Make a border of it on a buttered plate and fill the center with a marmalade made as follows: Cut the peeled stalks of a bunch of rhubarb into dice and allow them to simmer in a small amount of water till they are of the consistency of marmalade. Add three or four teaspoonfuls of sugar, a lump of butter and the rind of a lemon. Take from the fire and immediately add the beaten yolks of two eggs. Arrange, as stated, in the middle of the rice, sprinkle with a little more sugar and set m the oven for fifteen minutes or more before serving.

MENU 13

Potage à la Chicorée
Allumettes d'Anchois
Bœuf Bouilli en Vinaigrette
Pommes Maire
Salade de Tomates
Crème Brulée

Potage à la Chicorée.
Pick carefully and wash two or three heads of chicory, cut into shreds and pass through a little heated butter without allowing to take color. Then add sufficient of the water in which the Pommes Maire (below) were boiled to make the required quantity of soup, add pepper and salt, simmer for an hour. Just after taking from the fire add the beaten yolk of an egg. Pour into the tureen over toasted slices of stale bread.

Allumettes d'Anchois.
Make a fritter paste with flour and oil, omitting salt. Soften with white wine. Wash the desired number of anchovies, remove the bones and draw out the salt by soaking in milk. Dip into the paste and fry.

Boeuf Bouilli en Vinaigrette.
Cut cold, lean beef into narrow, thin slices. Place it in a bowl with a finely chopped onion and some chervil, a few cut-up gherkins, a teaspoonful of capers, pour oil, a little vinegar and the juice of half a lemon over, add pepper and salt, toss well together and serve at once.

Pommes Maire.

Use "kidney" potatoes if procurable; if not, ordinary potatoes of small size. Boil in salt water and peel while still hot, then cut in thick chips and place in a casserole and cover with boiling milk. Season with pepper and salt and allow to boil, turning with a fork till the milk has boiled away. Remove from the fire, pour over a cup of rich milk, season again and serve.

Salade de Tomates.

Cut a pound of not too ripe tomatoes into one inch cubes, add salt, pepper, vinegar and oil to taste and then toss together with a minced onion. Serve right away. If desired, cold boiled beef in dainty slices may be added.

Crème Brulée.

Blend a tablespoonful of flour with the yolks of three eggs and place in a casserole. Pour slowly in a pint or more of milk, add a pinch of cinnamon, a few drops of extract of lemon or any flavor desired, and stir constantly over the fire. When the cream is cooked, make a caramel sauce in a porcelain pot by melting five or six lumps of sugar and cooking to the browning point. Pour this into a serving dish, pour the cream over it and allow to cool.

MENU 14

Bisque d'Herbes
Turbot à la Rachel
Choufleur au Gratin
Salade Barbe de Capucin
Gâteau de Frangipane

Bisque d'Herbes.
Chop together about a handful each of
lettuce, sorrel, spinach, also a small onion,
a little celery and some chervil and cook all
with an egg sized piece of butter for fifteen
minutes, stirring constantly. Then add three
tablespoonfuls of flour made smooth with
a little stock, stir in four cupfuls of the
cauliflower water (which you will have from
a recipe following) into which has been
beaten the yolk of an egg. Serve very hot with
croutons.

Turbot à la Rachel.
Boil the fish in salted water. Whitefish or
haddock will serve as well as turbot. Make
the following sauce: Smooth and brown
together two tablespoonfuls of flour and
two ounces of butter and stir in five gills of
water in which the fish was boiled, adding
a teaspoonful each of anchovy essence and
mushroom catsup. Remove from the fire and
beat in the yolks of two eggs and the juice
of one lemon. Color with liquid carmine or
a few drops of cochineal and pour over the
fish.

Choufleur au Gratin.

Dip the cauliflower into ice water, then plunge it into boiling salted water to cook fifteen minutes. Cut a slice off the stalk, remove the leaves, lay on a flat dish and cover with a cream sauce. Sprinkle with grated breadcrumbs and grated Parmesan cheese, brown in the oven and serve.

Salade Barbe de Capucin.

Lay the stalks of American endive in a dish and cut into small pieces a medium shallot. Mix, add a French dressing and sprinkle with finely chopped tarragon leaves.

Gateau de Frangipane.

Whisk together a quarter of a pound of powdered sugar and the whites of three eggs, then beat in three tablespoonfuls of milk, the grated peel of a lemon and a dash of salt. Then stir in half a pound of flour. Bake in patty tins and when done scoop a piece out of the top of each patty and fill with jam. Then pour over a sauce made as follows: Put two wineglassfuls of white wine into a small saucepan and stir in a cupful of orange marmalade with the juice of a lemon. Thicken with a little corn-starch.

MENU 15

Potage Bisque
Canard à la Pertinset
Pommes de Terre à la Crème
Choufleur au Beurre Noir
Salade de Lentilles
Pêches au Vin

Potage Bisque.
Boil as many crabs as are needed in water, adding salt, pepper, two good sized onions and equal quantities of carrots and chives. Remove the crabs and take the meat from the claws. Mash the vegetables until they form a puree and add a good-sized lump of butter. Place over the fire with water or bouillon and allow to come to a boil. Serve very hot with croutons and the meat from the crab claws.

Canard à la Pertinset.
Place a carefully prepared duck in a casserole and dredge it with a lump of melted butter, add two onions, one clove, a dash of garlic. Put in the oven but do not allow the onions to become too brown before removing the duck. Then add five or six tomatoes, one glass of white wine, a glass of bouillon, a few cloves and a bayleaf. Let this boil over a low fire, then mash the tomatoes and onions, put back the duck into the casserole and boil for forty minutes.

Pommes de Terre à la Crème.
Put into a casserole a lump of butter, a pinch of flour, salt and pepper, nutmeg and a young onion. Mix well and add a cup of rich milk. Place on the fire, stir constantly, and remove as soon as the mixture comes to a boil. Meanwhile boil as many potatoes as are required in salted water. Peel and cut into slices, add to the sauce and serve.

Choufleur au Beurre Noir.

Boil a cauliflower and drain. Add a pinch of salt, nutmeg and a dash of vinegar to a pint of the water in which the cauliflower was cooked. Melt two tablespoonfuls of butter and when it is a light brown add it to the mixture. Pour over the cauliflower on a hot platter.

Salade de Lentilles.

Having boiled two cupfuls of lentils till they are tender, season them either hot or cold with a little garlic cut up fine, or with chives and serve in lettuce leaves with a French dressing.

Pêches au Vin.

Put peaches into a stewpan and cover them with water. In ten minutes remove the skins. Then place them in a shallow dish and cover them either with Madeira or Moselle wine and allow them to stand for at least two hours. Then drain them, place them in the dish in which they are to be served and cover them with vanilla sugar. Set the wine in which they have been soaked on the fire, add sugar to taste, and pour the sauce boiling over the peaches.

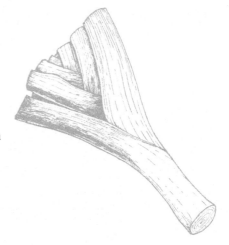

MENU 16

Sardines Grillées
Chapon à l'Indienne
Pommes de Terre en Matelote
Salade Beaucaire
Crème Fouettée

Sardines Grillées.
Grill half a dozen sardines, or as many as desired, for a few minutes. Melt butter in a frying-pan, stir in a little flour and moisten with hot water, then add a few drops of vinegar a dash of mustard, salt and pepper. Pour this very hot over the sardines.

Chapon à l'Indienne.
Prepare and truss a capon as for roasting, rub all over with butter and place in a casserole with a good-sized slice of salt pork. Cook over a slow fire for three hours. In the meantime, cook a cupful of rice, season it with a little curry powder and pimento, and place around the capon on the platter on which it is served.

Pommes de Terre en Matelote.
Slice freshly boiled potatoes and cook en casserole with seasoning of pepper and salt, two or three sliced onions, a sprig of chopped parsley, a lump of butter and a small amount of flour and water. Cook till all the ingredients are well blended and when heaped on a platter and ready for the table, pour over a glass or two of wine.

Salade Beaucaire.

Chop coarsely celery and endive together,
season with oil, vinegar and mustard an
hour before using. Just before taking to
the table, add chopped boiled ham, a
sour apple, diced, moistened with a little
tarragon and mayonnaise. Surround the
salad with a border of small potatoes, boiled
and sliced, alternated with slices of beet.

Crème Fouettée.

Whip cream till it is very thick or make
about a quart of custard. Mash thoroughly
a pound of cherries or raspberries, or both
with powdered sugar. Mix with the cream
or custard, beat again and serve immediately. In summer this may be iced with good
results.

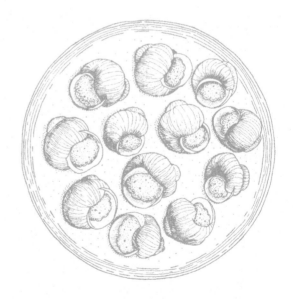

MENU 17

Potage Macédoine
Homards et Champignons
Côtelettes de Mouton à la Brunoise
Petits Pois à la Française
Choux à la Crème

Potage Macédoine.
Place thin pieces of ham in the bottom of a saucepan and then put in three each of turnips, potatoes and onions, all cut up small. Pour in some stock, season with pepper and salt and simmer till the ham and vegetables are cooked. Add a quart of milk and bring almost to a boil, strain and serve immediately.

Homards et Champignons.
Cut an equal quantity of lobster meat and mushrooms into dice. Boil some veloute" sauce together with some essence of mushrooms till somewhat reduced, then thicken and mix with the lobster and mushrooms. Fill ramekin cases with the preparation, sprinkle with breadcrumbs, pour over a little melted butter and bake in the oven till browned. Serve piping hot.

Côtelettes de Mouton à la Brunoise.

Trim mutton cutlets neatly, cutting away all fat, and place side by side in a large stewpan. Cover with well-flavored stock and leave to simmer, well covered, for an hour and a half. Take equal quantities of turnips, onions and celery and double the amount of carrots, cut all into quarter-inch cubes and fry in butter till they begin to color, putting in first the carrots, then the celery, then the onions and last the turnips. When all are done, drain and allow them to simmer gently in a little common stock. A little while before the cutlets are done drain off all the surplus stock from the vegetables, or boil it down quickly over a hot fire. Dress the cutlets on the rim of a platter, heap the vegetables in the center and pour the gravy all over them. Accompany with mashed potatoes.

Petits Pois à la Française.

Cook a pint of shelled peas till tender, drain and place on the back of the fire with not quite a gill of the water in which they have been boiled, a little flour and an ounce of butter. Simmer for five minutes, adding pepper and salt to taste and just before taking from the fire add the yolk of an egg mixed with a tablespoonful and a half of cream. Serve very hot in china or paper cases.

Choux à la Crème.

Put a small piece of butter in a saucepan with half a pint of water, a teaspoonful of sugar, a piece of lemon peel and a little salt. Boil well together, stir in two table-spoonfuls of flour and stir till thick and cooked. Allow this paste to cool and then work into it two eggs and sufficient milk to make it thin enough to drop from a spoon. Heat lard in a deep-frying pan, not quite to the point of boiling, and with a spoon drop the paste into it in lumps about the size of a hen's egg. When slightly brown and well swollen, remove the cakes, drain them well, scoop out a little of the top of each to form a hollow and allow them to cool. Whip cream to a stiff froth and put a small amount into the hollow of each chou, arrange on a fancy dish and serve. The chou may be filled with jelly or preserves if preferred.

MENU 18

Potage à la Printanière
Paupiettes de Veau
Pommes de Terre, Maître
d'Hôtel
Salade de Laitue
Feuillantines

Potage à la Printanière.
Cut two carrots and one turnip into shapes with a vegetable scoop, simmer for twenty minutes in salted water, drain and place in a quart of the water in which the potatoes (in this same menu) were boiled. Add a handful of chiffonades, cook five minutes and serve.

Paupiettes de Veau.
Cut thin cutlets from a fillet of veal and beat them fiat and even. Also mince a small quantity of the veal very fine, mix it with some of the kidney fat, also minced fine, and half a dozen minced anchovies, adding a little salt, ginger and powdered mace. Place this mixture over the slices of veal and roll them up. Beat up an egg, dip the rolled slices in it and then in sifted breadcrumbs. Let them stand for fifteen or twenty minutes, egg them again, roll in breadcrumbs and fry to a golden brown in boiling lard or clarified dripping, or stew them in some rich gravy with half a pint of white wine and a small quantity of walnut pickle.

Pommes de Terre, Maître d'hôtel.

Cut up carefully selected, underboiled and cold potatoes in rather thick slices. Dredge half a tablespoonful of flour in a saucepan with a lump of butter and when smooth add gradually a cupful of broth, stirring till it boils. Place in the potatoes along with a tablespoonful of chopped parsley and pepper and salt. Stew for three or four minutes, remove the pan to the side of the fire and add quickly the yolk of an egg previously well beaten with a teaspoonful of cold water and a little lemon juice. When the egg has become thickened, turn the potatoes with their sauce on a flat dish and serve.

Salade de Laitue.

Select fine lettuces, remove the coarse outer leaves, wash and wipe, place in a salad bowl and sprinkle over a tablespoonful of chopped chives, half a teaspoonful each of chopped chervil and tarragon. Season with a pinch of salt, half a teaspoonful of pepper, two tablespoonfuls of vinegar and a table-spoonful and a half of oil. Mix thoroughly and serve.

Feuillantines.

Prepare some puff paste; roll out to about a third of an inch thick and cut into strips an inch wide and two inches long. Spread a baking dish thick with butter, arrange the pieces of paste on it, placing them upon their sides and leaving a small space between them. Put them in the oven and when they are firm and their sides have spread, glaze them with white of egg and dust with powdered sugar. As the feuillan-tines are cooked set them on paper and drain off any extra grease. Now mask them separately with small quantities of different colored jams. Arrange on fancy edged dish-paper or a folded napkin on a dish and serve.

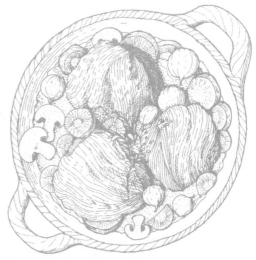

MENU 19

Potage Crème d'Orge
Bœuf à la Mode
Pommes de Terre, Sautées
Salade de Romaine
Soufflé au Chocolat

Potage Crème d'Orge.

Mix in a saucepan a teacupful of barley, an onion, a small piece of cinnamon, half a blade of mace and three pints of water in which potatoes have been boiled. When the mixture boils remove from the center of the fire and allow to simmer slowly for three hours or more. Pass through a fine sieve and return to saucepan. Mix in two tablespoonfuls of butter and half a pint of boiling milk, season with pepper and salt. Beat an egg yolk in a teacupful of milk, mix in the soup but do not allow to boil after egg is added. Serve with croutons.

Bœuf à la Mode.

Take the under part of a round of beef, place it in a deep earthen dish and pour over it spiced vinegar. Let the meat remain in this for several hours, then dress it with strips of salt pork, a third of an inch square, inserted in incisions made a few inches apart. Stuff larger incisions with breadcrumbs highly seasoned with salt, pepper, onions, thyme and marjoram. Bind the beef into a shape to retain the dressing and dredge with flour. Then cut up two onions, half a carrot and half a turnip and fry in fat drippings till brown and place in a stewpan. Brown the meat all over with the same fat, place on a trivet in the pan, half cover with boiling water, add a small quantity of mixed herbs tied in a bag, cover and simmer for about four hours, or till done. Take out carefully, remove strings and cloth, and place on a large dish. Skim off the fat from the gravy, add more seasoning, thicken with wetted flour worked smooth, boil for eight or ten minutes and strain over the meat. Decorate with small onions and potato balls.

Pommes de Terre, Sautées.

Boil potatoes until almost done, cut into quarters or slices of medium thickness. Melt butter or clarified drippings in a frying pan, put in the potatoes sprinkled with salt and pepper and finely chopped parsley and toss over the fire till they are a fine golden brown color. Serve with chopped parsley.

Salade de Romaine.

Put crisp leaves of romaine in a salad bowl rubbed lightly with a shallot or new onion. Make the following dressing. Take one hard-boiled egg and mash it as finely as possible with a fork, add a little paprika, a pinch of salt, half a teaspoonful of French mustard, a teaspoonful of hashed chives, the same of hashed tarragon, two tablespoonfuls of oil and three of vinegar. Add this to the romaine, toss well and serve.

Soufflé au Chocolat.

Mix a small tablespoonful of starch with a gill of milk and when quite smooth add two ounces of powdered sugar and two ounces of butter. Put the mixture into a saucepan and stir over the fire till it boils. When cold stir in an ounce of grated chocolate and the yolks of two eggs. Beat well together till perfectly smooth, then mix in the whites of the eggs. Pour into a buttered souffle dish and bake for forty minutes.

MENU 20

Potage Gourmet
Eglefin à la Maître d'Hôtel
Pommes de Terre, Casserole
Salade de Tomates et de Laitue
Canards Sauvages, Sauce Orange
Soufflé au Citron

Potage Gourmet.
Pour into a saucepan about a quart of the water in which potatoes have been boiled, add a small amount of cold chicken cut in small dice, two tablespoonfuls of boiled rice, two tablespoonfuls of cooked green peas and one truffle cut into dice, also pepper and salt, along with one or two whole cloves. Bring to a boil, allow to simmer for fifteen minutes, and serve.

Eglefin à la Maître d'Hôtel.
Cut a cleaned haddock open at the back on each side of the bone, duct with pepper and salt, dip in flour, place on a gridiron over a clear fire and cook for about twenty minutes, turning carefully from time to time. Remove from the fire, place two ounces of butter on the back of the fish, place it in the oven to melt the butter, then, put the fish on a hot platter and sprinkle with mince parsley and lemon juice, the latter heated.

Pommes de Terre, Casserole.
Boil a pound or two of potatoes, drain and mash and make into a stiff paste by adding butter and milk together with a little salt. Form into a casserole, put on a dish, make an opening in the top, brown in the oven and serve.

Salade de Tomates et Laitue.

Split the white leaves of lettuce into quarters and place in a bowl. Cut tomatoes into thin slices and place over the lettuce. Season with a sauce made of one part of vinegar, two of oil, a little salt and pepper. Pour the sauce over just before serving.

Canards Sauvages, Sauce Orange.

Roast two wild ducks over a brisk fire, having them underdone, more or less, according to taste. Baste all the time they are cooking with butter and the juice of lemon and serve with the following sauce. Shred finely the rind of two oranges and parboil in a little water. Melt an ounce of butter and stir into it a dessertspoonful of flour moistened with a little water. Stir well over the fire and then add the juice of the two oranges, some very clear gravy, flavor with pepper and salt and cayenne, then add the parboiled orange rind. Let the sauce boil and keep hot till wanted.

Soufflé au Citron.

Put three egg yolks and three ounces of powdered sugar into a basin with the grated rind of a lemon and a half and stir till quite thick. Add slowly a tablespoonful of lemon juice and then, quickly, the well beaten whites of the three eggs. Pour into a pie dish and bake in a medium oven for twenty minutes. When the surface is a golden brown it is done. Serve immediately.

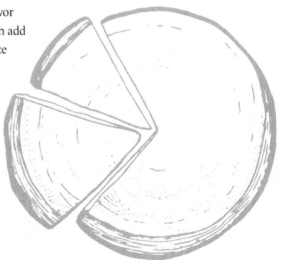

MENU 21

Filets de Carrelets, Italienne
Pommes de Terre, Loulou
Cailles Rôtis
Salade des Tomates et
d'Artichauts
Vol-au-Vent, Chantilly

Filets de Carrelets, Italienne.
Take the fillets of two firm flounders, trim
and flour each piece lightly. Dip in egg beaten
with pepper and salt, cover on both sides
with stale breadcrumbs and fry in boiling
olive oil. When the fillets are a golden brown
place on a sieve in front of the fire with a soft
paper beneath them that they may drain.
Serve with fried parsley and quarters of
lemon.

Pommes de Terre, Loulou.
Chop raw potatoes fine and place them in
a saucepan with butter and a seasoning of
pepper, salt, paprika and a trace of nutmeg.
Cover and cook very slowly, agitating them
constantly. When they become soft, beat
well and arrange a layer on a vegetable
dish, sprinkle with Parmesan cheese, put on
another layer of potatoes, then more cheese,
and so on, having the top layer of cheese.
Pour over all melted butter and bake about
twenty minutes in a slow oven.

Cailles Rôtis.
Tie a thin slice of bacon over the breast
of each quail, roast them at a clear fire for
fifteen minutes, basting frequently. Lay them
on crisp buttered toast, sprinkle with minced
parsley, salt and paprika, and serve with a
rich wine jelly on a separate dish.

Salade des Tomates et d'Artichauts.
Cut the under part of boiled artichokes into slices and take the same number of slices of tomato. Dip both into a dressing made of olive oil, vinegar, tarragon, chervil, salt and pepper, with a little mustard and arrange in a salad bowl. Pour over the remainder of the dressing and serve.

Vol-au-Vent, Chantilly.
Roll a pound of puff paste to about an eighth of an inch in thickness and cut out about thirty rounds with a fluted cutter, about two and a half inches in diameter. Then cut out the center of these with a cutter about an inch across. Roll out the paste taken from the centers and cut out more rings in the same way. Brush the rings over with egg, place one on top of another, two by two, press together so that they will stick, place on a baking sheet, brush over with egg and bake in a brisk: oven. When almost done sprinkle with sugar and allow to remain in the oven till they are glazed and fully done. Remove and place on a warmed platter and fill with any sort of cream desired, or jam or tart marmalade.

MENU 22

Potage Julienne
Homard Bordelaise
Canard à la Reine
Salade à la Russe
Café Bavaroise

Potage Julienne.

Cut carrots, onions, leeks and turnips into thin slices or strips of equal size with a head of celery. Put all into two ounces of butter melted in a saucepan and toss over a slow fire for a few minutes. If desired other vegetables in season such as cauliflower, peas or asparagus may be added. Pour clear chicken broth over the vegetables, put in some pieces of cold chicken, allow to come to a boil, then simmer till the vegetables are tender and pour the whole into the tureen with sippets of toast.

Homard Bordelaise.

Cut a small carrot and an onion into fine pieces and boil for five minutes in a wine-glassful of red wine. Now add the meat from two lobsters, cut in small pieces, say, about a pound and a half. Season with a very little pepper, salt, and a trace of nutmeg, adding, just before the lobster is cooked, about half a pint of velouté sauce. Stew well together and serve at once.

Canard à la Reine.

Cut off one wing of a duck and half the breast from the same side, remove the skin, take out the bone and fill the place with quenelle forcemeat. Lard the breast and put it into a braising pan over slices of leeks, carrots and onions and a little thyme, chervil, bayleaves and lemon peel. Add sufficient stock to prevent burning, set the pan on the fire and braise the duck, then glaze it. Serve with a puree of beans for garnish.

Salade à la Russe.

Cut cold chicken and salmon into thin slices, arrange in a salad dish and mix with finely cut cooked asparagus heads, carrots and cauliflower, a few capers and a little caviare. The dressing is made with three parts of oil and one of vinegar, a little mustard and cayenne pepper and a tablespoonful of minced onion. Pour over the salad and stand on the ice till served.

Café Bavaroise.

Grind half a pound of green coffee, roast in a sugar boiler without burning it or even browning and soak a quart of milk with it for about an hour. Now stir into a cupful of flour a teaspoonful of castor sugar into which has been dropped a little vanilla extract, and a little salt. Stir this all in with the strained coffee-flavored milk, bring to a boil, remove from the fire and stir in the yolks, then the whites of three eggs, all beaten firm. Fill paper cases with the mixture, bake, sprinkle castor sugar over the tops and serve at once.

MENU 23

Huitres à l'Américaine
Bœuf à l'Aurore
Pommes de Terre, Lyonnaise
Salade Française
Crème à la Russe

Huitres à l'Américaine.
Place in a sauce bowl a heaped teaspoonful of salt, three-quarters of a teaspoonful of white pepper, a medium sized onion, chopped, and a teaspoonful of minced parsley. Mix lightly together along with a teaspoonful of olive oil, six drops of tobasco sauce, a little Worcestershire sauce and a gill of vinegar. Put a teaspoonful of this mixture on each raw oyster just before taking to the table.

Bœuf à l'Aurore.
Season two steaks of about three-quarters of a pound each (any ordinary cut will do) with salt and pepper, baste on either side with a little oil and broil over a brisk fire for six minutes. Place on a hot dish and serve with the following sauce poured over: Mix in a saucepan a small glass of mushroom liquor with half a pint of bechamel sauce, half an ounce of butter and two or three tablespoonfuls of tomato sauce. Place on the fire, stir for ten minutes and just before removing add whole mushrooms cut in squares.

Salade Française.

Chop fine a bunch of parsley, two small onions and six anchovies. Lay them in a bowl and mix with salt and mustard to taste, two tablespoonfuls of salad oil and a gill of vinegar. Stir all well together and then add, one at a time, some very thin strips of cold roasted or boiled meat, not more than three or four inches long. Shake the slices well in the dressing. Cover the bowl closely and allow to stand for at least three hours. Serve garnished with parsley.

Pommes de Terre, Lyonnaise.

Cut into round slices eight boiled potatoes, lay them in a frying pan with an ounce and a half of butter and the slices of a partly cooked onion. Season with salt and pepper and cook till the potatoes become well browned, tossing all the while. Serve with chopped parsley sprinkled over.

Crème à la Russe.

Put into a saucepan a pint of milk, half a pound of lump sugar, the grated rind of two lemons and an ounce of gelatine, previously soaked in water. Cook till the sugar dissolves over a slow fire, then allow the mixture to cool somewhat before stirring in the yolks of two eggs, unbeaten. Place on the fire to curdle. Strain, and when cool add the juice of the two lemons and the whites of the eggs beaten stiffly. Stir all well together and pour into a wet mould. Turn out when well set.

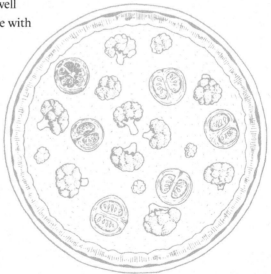

MENU 24

Potage Napolitaine
Truites à la Monbarry
Croquettes de Pommes de Terre
Celeri-rave en Salade
Pouding aux Figues

Potage Napolitaine.
Boil in strong bouillon small forcemeat balls made of any left-over game or meat. Then soak croutons in the same bouillon. Add the forcemeat balls and serve.

Truites à la Monbarry.
Prepare several trout and lay them in a pan with a quarter pound of butter and some strong spices. Allow to heat slowly in an open oven and when the butter is entirely melted, drop on the trout two well beaten yolks of eggs. Grate cheese over this and cover all with a quantity of fine breadcrumbs. Brown lightly in a hot oven and serve.

Croquettes de Pommes de Terre.
Boil and drain about two and a half pounds of potatoes. Add a generous quantity of butter, yolks of two eggs, salt and pepper and the white of the eggs beaten to a snow. Beat the whole up briskly, shape the mixture into balls and fry in a pan.

Celeri-rave en Salade.

Trim carefully a bunch of celery, leaving
on as much of the root as possible. Cut in
half and boil in salted water till tender.
Then trim into even sticks and season it
very piquantly with French mustard, a
few young onions, pepper, salt and finely
chopped parsley. Garnish with lettuce leaves
and slices of beet.

Pouding aux Figues.

Mix in a large bowl a cupful of breadcrumbs, half a cup of farina, a pinch of salt,
a cup of suet, cut fine, a cup of powdered
sugar, a minced carrot and a cup and a half
of chopped figs. Grease a baking mould, line
it with whole figs, and empty the mixture
into it. Cook for four hours, the pan standing in water. Serve hot with a rum sauce.

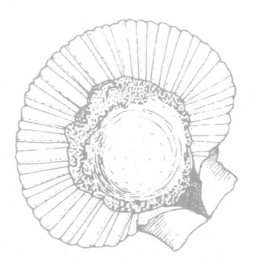

LET US
EAT FISH

CORA MOORE

Let Us Eat Fish:
A Famous French Luncheon à L'américaine

Only in the Latin countries has fish as an edible ever been fully appreciated and, as is the case with most other things gastronomic, it is in France that the food possibilities of the denizens of the water have been brought nearest perfection.

Over here we have always seemed to regard fish as useful chiefly for stocking aquariums or for furnishing sport for the vacationist, along with golf, tennis and bowling. True, we have become rather well acquainted with certain sea foods, the oysters, Blue Points and Cape Cods; we have a nodding acquaintance with some of the clam clan, especially the Rhode Island branch, and the Little Necks, the blue bloods of the family. And, of course, we are familiar with the crustaceans, the lobsters and the crabs.

And we know, too, certain succulent sea delicacies that come to us from Palm Beach shores and California and Oregon regions, tuna and halibut, bluefish and salmon as it comes to us variously prepared for the table. In short, we Americans are fairly friendly with a number of the aristocrats of the water, but on analyzing the situation we come to realize that as for knowing the "finny tribe" as a whole well enough to get complete gastronomic joy out of the situation, it remains that it is only the French people who are so blessed.

Time and the hour and the high price of meat, however, render it advisable, even absolutely necessary, that we work all our resources instead of only a part of them, to economize whenever and wherever we can, and the waters in our midst and around us are surely one of the most important resources not already worked to the limit.

Therefore, let us eat fish but first let us learn of the French about fish, even as we have learned of them concerning other foods, or as we have learned fashions, for, verily, the turning out of a proper fish dish for the table has ever been regarded by the French as no less an art than the creation of a beautiful frock in one of their ateliers. Moreover, their ways with fish are so broadly inclusive that one may make up an entire menu from one end to the other, with only a cup of coffee needed as a final fillip to make a perfect meal and all of fish.

By way of furnishing inspiration to our own appetites, herewith is a suggestion for a fish luncheon, a favorite menu of France, which its wealth and fashion delighted to have set before it in those good old days before the war. Substitutes are given for any fish not indigenous to American waters; otherwise, it is just as it would be served at one of the Riviera restaurants, with the exception, of course, that on the Riviera or at any of the noted marine restaurants, the visitor himself was permitted to select the fish for each course from among the different specimens swimming in the reserves, altogether unconscious of impending fate.

No French restauranteur worthy the name ever kept dead fish in stock, for nothing deteriorates so quickly. There is rarely over here the natural reserve that the Riviera takes as a matter of course, although there is, in some restaurants, the tank of running water in which the fish are kept in condition till required.

Let Us Eat Fish:

LUNCHEON MENU

Hors d'Œuvres. Little Necks or Blue Points.
At Monte Carlo one would be served Clovisses.

Lobster with Sauce Piquante.
A substitute for the French langouste, which is similar to a giant lobster minus the two long nippers. Or there might be served abroad for this course a little gelatinous fellow called supion, or sea-hedgehog, or perhaps nonnots, smaller and more delicate than our own whitefish.

French Sardines Grilled, or Shad Planked.
Shad is a most satisfactory substitute for the French restauranteur's delight loup de mer.

Flounder, Sauce Meunière, or Shrimps.
In Dieppe sole and certain crevettes are both specialties and are served at this juncture, but little sole is being received here and our own flounder answers requirements admirably. Shrimps, too, will please an American palate fully as well as the crevettes.

Bouillabaisse.
This, for which we have no nearer synonym than fish stew, which is a libel, is the piece de resistance of the luncheon. It is probably the most famous fish dish of France.

Salade de Poisson with Aioli.
Aioli is a Mediterranean mayonnaise and "the dressing," the French say, "is the soul of the salad."